MEMO FOR SPRING

MEMO FOR SPRING

50TH ANNIVERSARY EDITION

LIZ LOCHHEAD

Introduction by
ALI SMITH

This paperback edition published in Great Britain
in 2022 by Polygon, an imprint of Birlinn Ltd.

Birlinn Ltd
West Newington House
10 Newington Road
Edinburgh EH9 1QS

9 8 7 6 5 4 3 2

www.polygonbooks.co.uk

First published in 1972 by Reprographia.

ISBN 978 1 84697 610 0
EBOOK ISBN 978 1 78885 348 4

British Library Cataloguing-in-Publication Data
A catalogue record for this book is available
from the British Library.

Typeset in Verdigris MVB by Polygon, Edinburgh

Printed and bound in Great Britain by Clays Ltd, Elcograf S.p.A.

In memory of my husband, Tom Logan

CONTENTS

Preface ix
Introduction Ali Smith xix

Revelation 3
Poem for Other Poor Fools 5
How Have I Been 7
On Midsummer Common 8
Fragmentary 10
The Visit 11
After a Warrant Sale 13
Phoenix 15
Daft Annie on Our Village Mainstreet 16
Obituary 18
Morning After 21
Inventory 22
Grandfather's Room 23
For My Grandmother Knitting 25
Something I'm Not 27
Poem on a Day Trip 28
Overheard by a Young Waitress 29
Notes on the Inadequacy of a Sketch 30
Letter from New England 32
Getting Back 36
Box Room 38
Song for Coming Home 40
George Square 41

Man on a Bench 43
Carnival 44
Cloakroom 46
The Choosing 47
Homilies from Hospital 49
Object 52
Wedding March 55
Riddle-Me-Ree 56
Memo to Myself for Spring 57

PREFACE

The photograph and title on the cover of this book are the same ones from the cover of my first collection of poems fifty years ago (fifty, jeez-o!) way back in 1972. In a very different time. Now here it is, this new fiftieth anniversary edition. A rare and amazing honour. And don't I know it.

The girl in that photograph simply wouldn't have believed this could possibly be happening. Well, when you're twenty-four you don't really think you'll be around in fifty years. Nor that you'd want to be.

I remember that I wasn't too sure about either title or cover at the time, but Gordon Wright, who published it (back then he was running the one-man-band independent, Edinburgh-based imprint Reprographia, specialising in poetry) definitely was. He and Norman MacCaig convinced me – and they must have been getting something right. It hit a nerve, this first wee book of mine. Changed my life, too.

I look so demure, though, with those downcast eyes, and I wasn't ever that. And, in black and white, sweeter-looking, bonnier by far than I was in real life. I remember a distinguished Scottish critic telling me how, from seeing the cover of the book, how much he had fancied me before he'd ever met me and how disappointed he was when he actually did. Although even at the time I, silently, gave him nothing-out-of-ten for his non-chat-up line and for his quite un-asked-for honesty, I just thought 'fair enough really', and didn't bother (well, in those days it just wouldn't have been *done*) to tell him he would have had no chance anyway, I didn't fancy him either. So much for my career as a cover-girl.

Opening, in search of the girl who was not quite that girl on the cover, one of the four or five copies of *Memo for Spring* I still have on my shelves now – and I haven't opened one in quite a while – I find, behind the romantic packaging and the no-spine notebook-style binding, a scant thirty-two of the first things she had written and considered finished.

A few of them are very slight, song-like slightly melancholic love, and out-of-love, lyrics (well, I went to Glasgow School of Art from 1965–1970, where, as I always say, I specialised in Drawing and Painting and unrequited love) but more than half of the poems in here can still surprise me with their freshness and directness. Especially the ones which have caught something of that particular time, that place, the coal bing scarred industrial landscape with its red-sky-at-night of Motherwell's Ravenscraig blast-furnaces and the characters that belonged to that Lanarkshire mining village with its new-build, post-war, nineteen-fifties housing scheme attached to it, and the family I grew up in. And was putting behind me – *she's leaving home* – as I wrote.

Was I aware of that at the time? I'm not sure, but I do remember that this impulse to write these things had come from who knows where? And initially was not connected to any ambition or desire to see them in print; was always to me something that was all-my-own, my freedom. Simple as that.

Fundamentally I think to this day I feel exactly the same – ageless, genderless, free – whenever, prompted by some already existing quirk of language that's irking me, coupled with some as-yet wordless ghost of an idea, I can get going on something no one has asked me to write, something without deadline or purpose.

I still relish more than anything in my life that precious, and devoid of loneliness, alone-ness.

But I couldn't begin now to write the things the girl on the cover wrote then. Couldn't write with the careless confidence she had. She and I are in many ways quite different people. How could we not be after fifty years? Life goes past so very quickly, and, as the old will tell the young, the paradox is – with, on the surface, less happening in your life – weirdly, time does seem to keep on ever-accelerating, really does go faster the older you get. Even if you get the full three-score-and-ten, life is so short. And yet there are so many interestingly different bits to it. You'd never run out of things to write about.

How did the publication of *Memo for Spring* come about?

It wasn't something I strove for. I'm sorry to say I didn't have the manuscript of a collection of poems ready that I was sending out to publishers, stoically collecting rejection slips and doggedly finding another address of another possible publisher in *The Writers' & Artists' Yearbook*, trying again. It was a matter of my having the luck to be one of two supporting-artist poets opening for Norman MacCaig at his reading at an amazing all-day festival of poetry called *Poem 72* at the David Hume Tower of Edinburgh University. Hundreds – I am not exaggerating – honestly, hundreds of people turned up, young and long-haired in velvet loons or tweedy, academic, and middle-aged, all sorts of people and all-for-poetry on a cold Saturday in February 1972. Enthusiasts. Everybody wanted to hear Norman MacCaig. Of course. The biggest lecture theatre in the building was crammed to standing room only. I had just, backstage in the fug of the smoke-wreathed poets' greenroom, met, met in person, a hero of mine for the very first time.

I had discovered MacCaig for myself at the age of nineteen on the poetry shelves of the public library (unbelievably as it seems now, I had gone through secondary school without being introduced to the work of any Scottish poet except Burns) and the shelf of slender hardback phoenix-patterned covers of those Chatto & Windus volumes of MacCaig's, only two at a time as allowed – *Rings on a Tree, Riding Lights, A Round of Applause, A Common Grace, The Sinai Sort* – they were constantly borrowed by me, returned, fines paid, borrowed again all through that autumn and winter of 1968.

And now at *Poem 72* the organiser was saying, 'Do fifteen minutes, and, Norman, you do twenty-five.'

'No,' murmured Norman to me, 'you'll do twelve and I'll do twenty. Always leave them wanting more.' And he winked.

My bit passed in a blur and I was back in my seat in the front row for the first time listening, not reading from the page, to MacCaig. That voice, that timing. A masterclass in the art of performing poetry out loud.

Later that day a man I had never met before called Gordon Wright came up to me, told me he was a publisher, had enjoyed what I read at Norman's event and asked me did I have more poems, did I have a collection ready?

I wasn't sure about that, but my friend Alasdair Gray had recently received a small Arts Council grant and, typical Alasdair, to him a windfall like that ought to benefit other impecunious friends of his, too. He'd think of all sorts of ways to help emerging writers or artists whose work he was enthusiastic about and because he'd thought they were worth something, Alasdair had actually paid for the typist he always used to type up my poems. Clean copies. Essential. I'd tinkered, finalised and proofed and now they'd been impeccably typed on stencils, skins, that could be, by some now antique process, duplicated. (The words 'cyclostyling' and 'Gestetnering' come to my mind.) I had been allowed to run copies off in the school office at lunchtimes. (I was then in my first year as one of the worst rookie art teachers any comprehensive secondary school has ever had to put up with.)

In answer to Gordon's query: yes, I had copies of everything I considered finished. And I sent them to him.

Can it really be true that it only took about a week for him to get back to me? Gordon told me that he would like to publish a book of these poems – yes, in a few weeks' time, his printer had a fast turnaround, he had just made the deadline for the meeting of some committee, submitted my poems and already secured an Arts Council grant to make this happen.

There were only thirty-two poems – should we have waited a bit? Should I have produced some more work first? No, out it came, so slim a volume that it was bound like a notebook, without a spine. I have always bridled if anyone calls it 'your pamphlet' though. It was my first *collection*, I am adamant about that. And in its own small way, it was a big hit.

The first print run was an optimistic 1,500 copies. Gordon's energy and commitment to getting it out there, which was considerable, I owe so much to him, meant that his first edition of *Memo* had sold out, already making it – for poetry at least – a bestseller, and it was already reprinting a couple of months later. The 3,500 further copies (with the price raised from the initial 75p to 95) sold out gradually over the next four or five years.

Mainly here in Scotland. Where at that time there had been a dearth of women writing poems – no, that is not right, there *were* a very few very good women poets at that time (I've been reading some recently, they were undervalued) – but it's true that there was a distinct lack of women *being published* and so there was a genuine hunger for the female voice.

Not just here of course. The times indeed were a-changing.

Nothing else of mine ever will set the heather on fire like my first collection and I wonder why it did. Looking at it now I see nothing stridently or transgressively feminist here – all I was doing was writing from my own female point of view, what else was I going to do? But within the then all-male world of Scottish poetry, it was a one-off. It was *fresh*. And it was just my luck it being bang-on, so timely.

It was popular. Schools took it up. I'd be invited in to read to the non-academic early school leavers, especially the girls, by teachers who'd tell me they were doing MacCaig and Morgan with the clever boys in the fifth-year Highers classes. (I wasn't offended, just quite pleased and proud that for some of them when they heard this stuff, the sense of recognition they felt, their own everyday experience being reflected in my work might open them to more challenging poetry.) I'd get to read my poems on radio. They made a programme on a niche STV arts programme about me. Organisers of poetry readings and literary festivals would put on any three from a pool of about a dozen male poets, and me.

I realise how much I benefited from being just about the only female poet around.

Over the years I have become aware that my early work was particularly meaningful to women, especially to certain younger women – they've told me so, even said so publicly – as they began to write.

A writer like you Ali Smith, the amazing and wonderful Ali Smith, so puckish, profound and absolutely original, has said my wee book was an inspiration to her. The incredibly prolific Ali Smith – wow, there are over a dozen Ali Smith books on my bookshelves, novels (oh, your whole time-obsessed, *now*-obsessed, quartet of seasons, *Autumn, Winter, Spring, Summer)* and my favourite short stories, I've read every single thing you've written ever since *Free Love*, your first slim volume, way back in 1995 – and here you've actually written the introduction to this wee fiftieth anniversary edition of mine! Well, Ali, you would have been not quite ten years old when *Memo for Spring* came out, it couldn't have meant anything to you till you were, what, sixteen or seventeen at the earliest? . . . At that age it would have meant a hell of a lot to me, too, if I'd found a book of poems I really liked by someone young, and female, and Scottish, who had grown up in a council house like me. (I was perfectly all right though with Anon, and Keats, and Louis MacNeice. And eventually I did find Denise Levertov, Elizabeth Bishop and Joni Mitchell.)

I wish *I'd* written more, but with me how it's been is: the poem-making thing has often gone away for a while, and there hasn't been anything I could do about that till it came back.

As, so far, it always has.

'Through the process of examining my life, I thought I might understand myself better. One thing I have learnt is that, while I used to think I was making individual choices, now, looking back, I see clearly that I was following trends and general patterns of behaviour which I was about as powerless to resist as a migrating bird or a salmon swimming upstream.' These aren't my words. This is the biographer Claire Tomalin in the Introductory Note to her autobiography, *A Life of My Own*. (It's also a book, as it happens, with a photograph of a heart-breakingly young and open-faced girl on its cover, Tomalin as a student at Cambridge, I'd imagine.) I read and much enjoyed it recently, wondering if it is because I am getting older that I find myself reading so many more biographies and autobiographies, especially about women, women a generation older than I, silently comparing my life and my times with theirs? And yet I have a horror of nostalgia, that useless and cloying sentimental longing that bleeds life into the past. I know I would find writing out loud – directly and sans persona – about my own life unbearably painful. I don't know why.

OK: once upon a time there was this girl from Motherwell who had the nerve to write some poems.

Who did she think she was?

Well . . . she thought she was leaving Glasgow very soon and wouldn't be living there permanently again; she thought that she knew where she was going and who was going with her; she thought that she had given up on drawing and painting, that she'd gone to art school where she had somehow lost the urge to be any kind of visual artist, would not be persevering in that line; she thought she would never write anything longer than – or anything other than – a poem; she thought she would never, hell no, write anything in 'Scots'.

I'm glad to say it turned out she was completely wrong about each and every one of these things.

That was her then. Who am I? Now.

Well, I'm no spring chicken. I've just had my seventy-fourth birthday, and this is me now into my seventy-fifth year.

Which sounds seriously old. Do I feel it? Sometimes, not usually.

Not today. Thanks to Spotify and these rather tinny speakers on this computer of mine, at my desk as it's winter-darkening early, I'm letting you, Bob Dylan, serenade me from way back in 1965, tell me I've got everything I need, that I'm an artist and I don't look back, how you'll bow down to me on Sunday, salute me when my birthday comes, on Halloween buy me a trumpet and for Christmas get me a drum. As long as you keep singing out that I belong to you, I can almost believe that I'll never stumble, I've got no place to fall. Hey, I wish I could find me that famous Egyptian ring which at the moment I seem to have, oh, perhaps let's hope only temporarily, mislaid somewhere, Mr Octogenarian Zimmerman. Wish I too could sparkle before I speak, be more of that hypnotist collector than this walking antique, because getting back to where I once belonged has somehow proved incredibly hard, I don't know why. Try as I might, day and daily, as deadline after deadline has been missed, I just couldn't seem to get the tone, or the truth, of this right. Should have been easy. All I had to do was tell it like it was, as far as I can remember it, and try and paint some kind of picture of the aspiring wordsmith as a young woman.

All I'm hoping for, as I finally sign off on this preface, is to still be keeping on till the end of my days, experimenting, creating new things, drawing, painting, playing, making marks on paper, collaborating whenever I'm invited to do so with musicians, theatre-makers and other artists, because I love collaborative projects, have been lucky enough to work on a lot of them and would like to do more. But above all I'm hoping to never lose the special thrill of being a solitary still-aspiring wordsmith who has, on the go, what might, or might not, eventually become a poem.

INTRODUCTION

What does formative really mean?

It was 1979. I was sixteen. I lived in the Highlands, I was in fifth year at Inverness High School. I loved books. I was clever. I'd learned when to hide both these things. The world was all before me and already I knew the negotiations that we were meant to make, the compromises expected, and my own spirit champing at the bit.

One day our English teacher, Ann McKay, asked me would I babysit that Saturday night. Course I would. Cash in hand.

When the adults had gone out and the kids were asleep I went straight to the bookshelves, the evening spring light still hitting them, to check out one of my most inspiring teacher's books.

What was this? A slim stapled book too thin for its name to be on its spine.

Memo for Spring, it said on the cover. Then the writer's name. Liz Lochhead. Then a black and white photo of a girl, a young woman, pensive, thinking, she looked somehow complete, sitting in moorland or scrubland, countryside that looked real, not a cliché, that looked like home actually, and she looked like she was about to raise her eyes and speak, or had just spoken, just finished saying something and was about to speak again.

It was poems, a poetry collection.

I opened it at the first. 'Revelation'.

The poem was an unsettling and vivid one, about a small girl on a farm taken to have a look at the farm's bull.

I'd see when I'd read it years later that this poem's about a girl confronted for the first time in her life not just by the penned-up presence of nature but also the clearly gendered heft of mythic force. But when I first read it, aged sixteen, what I knew immediately was – and this has been a typical mark of Lochhead's work all through her life – that this poem about power was an answering power in itself.

More, this slight-seeming, almost casually told opener for *Memo for Spring* was written in an English somehow as Scottish as my own. It sank into me, recognition, direct connection, and I sat on the floor and read the book from start to end. Then I read it again.

Revelation all right. What I felt was a combination of astonishment, possibility and profound relief. A poet who's a woman, and a Scot! That you could be all three of these things! That it might be possible in the world to be anything like this poet who used language as clear, as everyday, as streetwise, as this, and as deceptively dimensional as deep water.

How do I sum up the impact that this book had on me? Not just on me, on us all. It's an impact the size of a changed world. Remember, this was a time now unimaginable, when if I'd tried to count on both hands the number of Scottish women writers we knew about, never mind had access to or had actually read, I'd have had the whole of one hand and some fingers of the other still going spare. One of the core reasons such a thing is now unimaginable is this book by this writer.

Memo for Spring let me and all its readers know in poem after poem and in its unpretentious, vital, naturally rhythmic, unforced, witty and questioning ways, that something else wasn't just possible, it was happening. I think now of the way the book and the writer broke the mould, and I reckon that the current richness of Scottish women's writing, that the richness of the writing of all the great late renaissance Scottish formal mould-breakers, and so much of the vital writing that's come out of Scotland (and not just Scotland) by writers of all the genders in all the forms in the past fifty years, will have had a taproot, knowingly or unknowingly, in what was made possible by this slim powerful debut.

Back in 1979 my teacher came home from her evening out and I held up the book and said, where can I get a copy of this? She told me she'd bought it when she'd seen Liz Lochhead read and speak at a festival in Edinburgh, and how good it had been. (A festival! Writers speaking and reading at one!) She lent me the book for a week.

I didn't have my own copy till into the early eighties, when Liz Lochhead came to Aberdeen where I was a student, she came with James Kelman and Alasdair Gray to read at an event, and all three writers read writing that blew our minds that night, making clear again what I'd felt when I opened *Memo for Spring* with no idea what its seeming slimness held – that in writing, and especially right then in Scottish writing, what was possible was anything, everything.

Memo. A written reminder, a brief-noted message to remind you what you need to know.

Spring. The start of things, the upward leap, the source.

I bought one of the (I think there were only two or three) copies of the original edition of *Memo for Spring* for sale that night in 1981. It cost 95p, quite a lot at the time, and I got it signed. By then, nearly a decade after its very small original print run, there can't have been many copies left in the world, and mine as it happens was one of a faulty print-run and had some blank pages where some of the poems should be. So I took it to the library and copied in by hand, careful to get the line ends and punctuation right, the missing poems.

Very Best Wishes, Liz Lochhead, my copy says on its inside first page in her own hand.

You're telling me. What luck, what vision, what liberation, what good chance readers had, and always will, to encounter this book, so wise and wry and warm and witty and clever and feeling and clear, and the new ground Liz Lochhead broke with it, and the life in it a threshold to all the futures.

Ali Smith

MEMO FOR SPRING

REVELATION

I remember once being shown the black bull
when a child at the farm for eggs and milk.
They called him Bob – as though perhaps
you could reduce a monster
with the charm of a friendly name.
At the threshold of his outhouse, someone
held my hand and let me peer inside.
At first, only black
and the hot reek of him. Then he was immense,
his edges merging with the darkness, just
a big bulk and a roar to be really scared of,
a trampling, and a clanking tense with the chain's jerk.
His eyes swivelled in the great wedge of his tossed head.
He roared his rage. His nostrils gaped like wounds.

And in the yard outside,
oblivious hens picked their way about.
The faint and rather festive jingling
behind the mellow stone and hasp was all they knew
of that Black Mass, straining at his chains.
I had always half-known he existed –
this antidote and Anti-Christ his anarchy
threatening the eggs, well rounded, self-contained –
and the placidity of milk.

I ran, my pigtails thumping on my back in fear,
past the big boys in the farm lane
who pulled the wings from butterflies and
blew up frogs with straws.
Past thorned hedge and harried nest,
scared of the eggs shattering –
only my small and shaking hand on the jug's rim
in case the milk should spill.

POEM FOR OTHER POOR FOOLS

Since you went I've only cried twice.
Oh never over you. Once
it was an old head at a bus window
and a waving hand.
Someone's granny, a careful clutcher of her handbag
and wearing a rainhat despite the fact
it wasn't raining. Yet
waving, waving to grandchildren already turned away
engrossed in sweets she had left them.
Old head. Waving hand.

> Oh she wasn't the type to expose herself
> to the vagaries of weather
> (a rainhat in no rain)
> Yet waving, waving to those who had already
>   turned away.

Then once it was a beggar by the pub doorway
and his naked foot.
Some drunk old tramp,
player of an out of tune mouthorgan
and begging. Instead of his cap,
his boot for alms.
His playing was hopeless,
his foot bare in the gutter in the rain,
his big boot before him, empty, begging.
Oh it was a scream. I laughed
and laughed till I cried.

It was just his poor
pink and purple naked foot
out on a limb
exposed.
And how (his empty boot) he got nothing
in return.

HOW HAVE I BEEN

since you last saw me?
Well,
        I've never been lonely
        I've danced at parties,
        and drunk flat beer
with other men;
        I've been to the cinema and seen
        one or two films you would have liked
with other men;
        I've passed the time in amusement arcades
        and had one or two pretty fruitless
        go'es on the fruit machine;
        I've memorised the patterns
        of miscellaneous neckties.
Indifferent, I
        put varying amounts of sugar
in different coffee cups
        and adjusted myself to divers heights
        of assorted goodnight kisses, but
my breasts (once bitten)
                shy away from contact
I keep   a curb
                on mind and body –
Love?   I'm no longer
                        exposing myself.

ON MIDSUMMER COMMON

On midsummer common
it's too good to be true,
backdrop of cricketers,
punts on the river,
the champ of horses
and mayflies in June
mere midsummer commonplace.

Not in midsummer,
but with the real rain of more normal weather
putting a different slant on things,
my hard edged steel town
seen through the blur of bus windows.
Saturday afternoon streets crammed
with shoppers laden under leaden skies.
Out of the constant comedown of the rain, old men
in the final comedown of old age
file into public libraries to turn no pages.
Saturday. My town
can't contain itself.
Roars rise and fall,
stadiums spill
football crowds in columns
in the teeming rain.
Saturday buses are jampacked with football rowdies
all going over the score.
I am overlapped by all the fat and laughing losers
that pour from bingo parlours.
Outside cinemas, steadies

queue steadily to buy
their darkness by the square foot.
The palais and troc are choc-full
of gaudy girls dressed parrot fashion.
Saturday's all
social clubs, singers, swilled ale.
So much is spilt –
the steel clang, the clash of creeds,
the overflow of shouts and songs,
the sprawl of litter,
the seep of smells,
the sweat, the vinegar, the beer –
so much slops
into that night nothing goes gentle into,
not even rain.
Such a town
I feel at home to be at odds with.

Here on midsummer common on
a midsummer Saturday
you, this day, this place and I
are just exchanging pleasantries.
Oh, it's nice here, but
slagheaps and steelworks
hem my horizons
and something compels
me forge my ironies from a steel town.

FRAGMENTARY

Twilight (six o'clock and
undrawn curtains). It's as if
                                        upstairs
                                                    from me
lives some crazy projectionist
running all his reels at once.
Pub-sign neon scrawls credits on the sky that's
cinemascope for him. He
treats me to so many
simultaneous
home movies, situation comedies, kitchen sink dramas
I can't make sense of them –
just snippets, snatches with the sound gone,
mouthings in a goldfish bowl.

THE VISIT

We did not really want to go,
not very much,
but he said it was our Christian Duty
and anyway he had already booked the bus.
So we went
despite ourselves
dreading, half hoping to be horrified.
Through corridors with a smell,
bile greenish-yellow unfamiliar smell
of nothing *we* knew,
but of oldness, madness, blankness,
apathy and disinfectant.
We grinned.
We did not know what else to do.
A grimace of goodwill and Christian greetings,
hymn books clutched in sweaty palms.
We are the Church Youth Club to sing to you,
bring you the joy we have never felt.
We passed on through the strange men –
complex simple faces
so full of blankness you would not believe it –
bowing, smiling, nodding they ignored us,
or acknowledged us with sullen stares.
A tall orderly came towards us
with eyes that couldn't keep still
and a nervous twitch.
I wonder had he always been like that,
the watcher, the keeper-
calm of what prowled his cage?

We sang. The minister shut his eyes
and prayed from unironic lips
with easy phrases.

For me, only an orderly
who prayed with his eyes skinned.
Just the flick of eyes
which *can't* be everywhere at once.

AFTER A WARRANT SALE

I watched her go,
Ann-next-door
(dry eyed,
as dignified
as could be expected)
the day after they came,
sheriff court men
with the politeness of strangers
impersonally
to rip her home apart –
to tear her life along the dotted line
officially.

On the sideboard that went for fifteen bob,
a photograph.
Wedding-day Walter and
Ann: her hair was lightened,
and heart, with hopes.
No one really knows
when it began to show –
trouble, dark roots.

It was common knowledge
there were faults on both sides,
and the blame –
whether it was over drink
or debt no one seems to know,

or what was owing to exactly whom.
Just in the end the warrant sale
and Ann's leaving.

But what seemed strange:
I wondered why,
having stayed long past the death of love
and the ashes of hope,
why pack it up and go
over some sticks of furniture
and the loss of one's only partially
paid-for washing machine?

Those who are older tell me,
after a married year or two
the comforts start to matter
more than the comforting.
But I am very young,
expecting not too much of love –
just that it should completely solve me.
And I can't understand.

PHOENIX

When crowsfeet get a grip on me
I'll call them laughter lines
I'll think of burnt-out romances
as being my old flames.

DAFT ANNIE ON OUR VILLAGE MAINSTREET

Annie
with your euphemisms to clothe you
with your not all there
        your sixpence short in the shilling
with your screw loose
        your crazy tick tock in the head
        your lurching pendulum
                                        slightly unbalanced
with your plimsolls in winter
with your big-boots in summer and
        your own particular unseasonal
        your unpredictable weather.

Annie
out of the mainstream
mainstreet Annie
down at the cross
with your religious mania
singing Salvation Army choruses
to all on Sunday.
Annie with your unique place
        your pride of place
        in the community –
how
        to every village
        its doctor and its dominie
        its idiot.

Annie
with the village kids afraid of you
with your myth of witchery
with your mystery
        your big raw bones
and   your hamfisted face.
with your touching every lamp-post
        your careful measured paces down mainstreet
clothed in euphemisms
and epithets.
Daft Annie
        your epitaph.

OBITUARY

We two in W2
walking,
and all the W2 ladies, their
hair coiffed and corrugated come
with well-done faces
from the hairdresser's.
We together
laughing,
in our snobbery of lovers,
at their narrow vowels
and strange permed poodles.
Locked too long in love, our eyes
were unaccustomed to the commonplace.
Seems silly now really.

We two in W2
walking
down Byres Road
passing unconcerned
a whole florist's
full of funerals,
the nightmare butcher's shop's
unnumbered horrors,
the hung fowls
and the cold fish
dead on the slab.
We saw ourselves duplicated
by the dozen in the chainstore
with no crisis of identity.

Headlines on newsagents' placards
caused us no alarm
Sandwichman's prophecies of doom
just slid off our backs.
The television showroom's window
showed us cities burning
in black and white but we
had no flicker of interest.
An ambulance charged screaming past
but all we noticed was the funny old
Saturday street musician.
Seems silly now really.

We two one Sunday
at the art galleries
looking only at each other.
We two one Sunday
in the museum –
wondering why the ownership of a famous man
should make a simple object a museum piece –
and I afraid
to tell you how
sometimes I did not wash your coffee cup for days
or touched the books you lent me
when I did not want to read.
Well, even at the time
that seemed a bit silly really.

Christmas found me
with other fond and foolish girls
at the menswear counters

shopping for the ties that bind.
March found me
guilty of too much hope.
Seems silly now really.

MORNING AFTER

Sad how
Sunday morning finds us
separate after all,
side by side with nothing between us
but the Sunday papers.
Held like screens before us.
        Me, the *Mirror*
reflecting only on your closed profile.
        You, the *Observer*
encompassing larger, other issues.
Without looking up
you ask me please to pass the colour section.
I shiver
while you flick too quickly
                        too casually through the pages, with
                        too passing
                        an interest.

INVENTORY

you left me
    nothing but nail
    parings orange peel
    empty nutshells half-filled
    ashtrays dirty
    cups with dregs of
    nightcaps an odd hair
    or two of yours on my
    comb gap toothed
    bookshelves and a
    you shaped
    depression in my pillow.

GRANDFATHER'S ROOM

In your room in the clutter of pattern
you lie.
Sunlight strains through lace curtains,
makes shadow patterns
on wallpaper's faded trellises,
on fat paisley cushions,
on the gingham table-cloth.
On the carpet, rugs
layer on layer like the years,
pattern on pattern,
cover the barest patches.
Geometric, floral, hand-made rag rugs,
an odd bit left over from the neighbours'
new stair carpet –
patterns all familiar
from other people's houses,
other people's lives.

In a clutter of patterns
you lie,
your shrunken head,
frail as a shell or a bird skull,
peeps from the crazy-paved
patch-work quilt.

Above your bed
in his framed death, your son,
my Uncle Robert that I never knew.
They say

he was well-known for his singing at weddings
and was a real nice lad, killed
in the war at twenty-one.
His photo, hung so long in the same place, has
merged with the wallpaper,
faded into the pattern.
(But it can't be moved now,
it has left its mark.)
Uncle Robert in a uniform
above your bedside table-top, the
medicines, the bright and bullet-shaped pills,
nothing in the angle of his smile
nor in the precise tilt of his cap, hinting
how soon, how suddenly he was to die.

There he is in black and white, believable.
Oh yes, he smiled and sang.
His sudden death stopped short
a slower certain dying, change.
While the other wall holds up
a scrap of nineteen thirty-three,
maintains it's true.
A photo of the family (or so they say) –
that flop-haired boy my balding father?
and you, grandfather, tall and strong,
smouldering in a landscape of shut pits and silent chimneys?
It's framed like a fact,
set fair and square but has less weight
is less real
than those faint patterns traced
by a weak sun through lace curtains.
Pale shadows, constantly changing.

FOR MY GRANDMOTHER KNITTING

There is no need they say
but the needles still move
their rhythms in the working of your hands
as easily
as if your hands
were once again those sure and skilful hands
of the fisher-girl.

You are old now
and your grasp of things is not so good
but master of your moments then
deft and swift
you slit the still-ticking quick silver fish.
Hard work it was too
of necessity.

But now they say there is no need
as the needles move
in the working of your hands
once the hands of the bride
with the hand-span waist
once the hands of the miner's wife
who scrubbed his back
in a tin bath by the coal fire
once the hands of the mother
of six who made do and mended
scraped and slaved slapped sometimes
when necessary.

But now they say there is no need
the kids they say grandma
have too much already
more than they can wear
too many scarves and cardigans –
gran you do too much
there's no necessity.

At your window you wave
them goodbye Sunday.
With your painful hands
big on shrunken wrists.
Swollen-jointed. Red. Arthritic. Old.
But the needles still move
their rhythms in the working of your hands
easily
as if your hands remembered
of their own accord the pattern
as if your hands had forgotten
how to stop.

familiar with, the tune
of their talking, comes tumbling before them
down the stairs which (oh I forgot) it was my turn
to do again this week.
My neighbour and my neighbour's child. I nod, we're not
on speaking terms exactly.

I don't know much about her. Her dinners smell
different. Her husband's a bus driver,
so I believe.
She carries home her groceries in Grandfare bags
though I've seen her once or twice around the corner
at Shastri's for spices and such.
(I always shop there – he's open till all hours
making good.) How does she feel?
Her children grow up with foreign accents,
swearing in fluent Glaswegian. Her face
is sullen. Her coat is drab plaid, hides
but for a hint at the hem, her sari's
gold embroidered gorgeousness. She has
a jewel in her nostril.
The golden hands with the almond nails
that push the pram turn blue
in this city's cold climate.

POEM ON A DAY TRIP

It's nice to go to Edinburgh.
Take the train in the opposite direction.
Passing through a hard land, a pitted
and pockmarked, slag-scarred, scraped land.
Coal. Colossus of pit-bings,
and the stubborn moors where Covenanters died.
Hartwood, Shotts, Fauldhouse, Breich –
something stirs me here
where the green veneer is thin,
the black-gut and the quarried ash-red
show in the gashes.
But the land changes
somewhere in the region of West and Mid Calder,
greener and gentler, rolling Lothians.
Edinburgh. Your names are grander –
Waverley, Newington, Corstorphine,
never Cowcaddens, Hillhead or Partick.
No mean city,
but genteel, grey and clean city
you diminish me –
make me feel my coat is cheap,
shabby, vulgar-coloured.
You make me aware of your architecture,
conscious of history and the way it has
of imposing itself upon people.
Princes Street.
I rush for Woolworth's anonymous aisles,
I feel at home here
you could be anywhere –
even in Glasgow.

OVERHEARD BY A YOUNG WAITRESS

Three thirty-fivish women met one day,
each well glossed against the others' sharp eyes for flaws.
Old school friends apparently – they slipped
with ease into the former conspiracy of dormitories, and
discussed over coffee and saccharine, the grounds
for divorce. All agreed love made
excessive demands on them,
wondered how long it must be missing
before it could be
                                        Presumed Dead.

NOTES ON THE INADEQUACY OF A SKETCH

at Millport Cathedral, March 1970

Fields strung out so, piece-
meal on a crude felt-tip line
in real life revealed ribs
where the plough had skinned them alive.
My scrawl took the edge off the dyke.
Sure. But omitted to mark how
it held together, the gravity
of the situation (it being
a huddle of rough stone forms in a cold climate)
how it was set to hump across hills, or at what
intervals over which stones exactly
snails had scribbled silver.
I jotted down how fence
squared up to dyke (but nothing of
the wool tufts caught on random barbs)
how it bordered on that
ridiculous scrap of grass
(but failed to record its precise
and peculiarly Scottish green).
I made a sheer facade
of the cruciform cathedral, stated
only that the rectory garden
slanted towards an empty greenhouse
on the graveyard's edge.
For gravestones, I set mere slabs right-
angling to a surface I took at face value.
(I did not explain how at my feet
sprawled a rickle of rabbit bones

ribcage and spine in splinters,
skull intact.) I probed no roots.
I did not trace either gravestones'
legends or their moss (it let me read
between the lines the stones' survivals).
I selected what seemed to be essentials.
Here, where wind and rain
made a scapegoat of a scarecrow, my pen
took it for an easy symbol. But it's plain
setting down in black and white
wasn't enough, nor underlining
certain subtleties. This sketch became
a simile at best. It's no metaphor.
It says *under prevailing conditions*
smoke from a damp bonfire was
equal to tonal value to the sea.
So what?
            Today on the empty
summer's sand the March rain needled no one.
(My sketch mentions no rain
neither how wet it was nor how straight
it fell nor that seagulls tried to call a halt
to it.) From my quick calligraphy of trees
no real loud rooks catcall the sea's
cold summersalt.

LETTER FROM NEW ENGLAND

from a small town, Massachusetts

I sip my coke at the counter
of the Osterville soda-fountain
that is also the Osterville news-stand, &
I watch Nothing Happening
out on mainstreet
of this small New England town.

just
the sun &
white clapboard houses with trees in between, &
certain cottonclad &
conservative spinsters nod at nodding acquaintances, &
occasional rocking chairs nod on front porches &
old men in panamas hail each other loudly, &
mothers compare feeding methods, &
the parson posts a letter &
some highschool kids are perched on the fence
        of the Pilgrim Fathers' Museum
        (open only on Sundays)
        practising real hard at sitting on fences so
        as to grow up to be
        realgood New Englanders, &
cars purr past, each containing
one pale lady in sunglasses
        behind a smoke-tinted windscreen
        in transit between
        Ideal Home
        and beautyparlour, &

what-looks-to-me like a farmer
        puts a Big Box
        in the back of a Ford, &
my-bike-without-a-padlock
        sits for hours outside the library
        because you can Sorta Trust Folk
        in a small New England town
        where no-one locks their doors.

        business is slow, says the soda-jerk,
        like molasses in janu-werry, &
        I buy myself a *New York Times*
        at the Osterville news-stand
        (that is also the soda-fountain)
        just to remind me that
        This is America, &
        America has Problems,
                        pollution &
                        recession &
                        escalation &
                        de-escalation &
                        women's liberation &
                        racial integration
                        which
        is not-to-speak-of Unspeakable Problems like
        Spiro T. Agnew
        & not-to-mention Problems
        like odorforming bacteria & horrid
        halitosis

        which as each &
        every ad would warn us are
        ever-ready to engulf us.

& I feel I should be somewhere else
like
        a be-in, or
        a love-in, or
        learning how the American Election System works, &
        How To Make A President &
        what *is* the difference between a
        republican & a
        dem-o-crat?

I should be
        spectating at a looting, or
        sightseeing in some ghetto, or
        marching civil-righteously, or
        rioting on campus &
        striking matches
        for people burning draftcards &
        sticking pink bubblegum
        on every seat in the senate
        as a last-ditch attempt
        at Nonviolent Action, or
        out in California
        getting genned-up generally
        on the Voice of Youth's current (& ∴ correct)

Attitudes
to the kinds of Grass & Peace & Love
different from the grass & peace
you get for free in New England with
No Attitudes Necessary.

I should be somewhere else –
not
practising Non Involvement
(& taking a slow suntan)
eavesdropping on the Silent Majority
(& eating hot butterscotch &
ice cream sundae
with marshmallow sauce vanilla
cream and double nuts)
at the Osterville soda-fountain
that is also the news-stand
in this small New England town.

GETTING BACK

I was to ring you, remember,
the minute I got back. (Your number
among all those American addresses that came since.)
        I look
it up where you wrote it, something special in my book. Four
months. Four thousand miles apart and more.
        Keeping in touch
with us both on the move and all, no fixed addresses,
        was too much
to ask of us. From the Acropolis to the Empire State
it's a far cry. Then, between San Francisco and
        Istanbul, late
August burned and the distance grew.
That close and now at odds. You
had done with the sun by the time I got round to it.
You woke up, I sank into sleep, worlds away. We moved
        in opposite
directions in the dark about each other's days.
Now, I only lift the telephone and the operator says
she's trying to connect us. Between us four miles,
        no distance,
it's a local call – I should get through for sixpence.

But I just got back. No small change. I forgot
to check on it. I push a quarter in the shilling slot,
pips stop (my heartbeat), you reply to my
        small and civic dishonesty.
I jingle my pocket – nickles, dimes,
        meaningless currency –

and try to picture you at the receiving end – moustache
          at the mouth-piece
unless you've changed a lot. I take a breath
          'And how was Greece?'
We namedrop cities into silences, feel the distance grow
find no common ground to get back to. I know
in my bones, nothing's the same anymore.
Don't you remember the girl I'm a dead ringer for?

BOX ROOM

First the welcoming. Smiles all round. A space
for handshakes. Then she put me in my place –
oh, with concern for my comfort. 'This room
was always his – when he comes home
it's here for him. Unless of course,' she said,
'He brings a Friend.' She smiled. 'I hope the bed
is soft enough? He'll make do tonight
in the lounge on the put-u-up. All right
for a night or two. Once or twice before
he's slept there. It'll all be fine I'm sure –
next door if you want to wash your face.'
Leaving me 'peace to unpack' she goes. My weekend case
(lightweight, glossy, made of some synthetic
miracle) and I are left alone in her pathetic
shrine to your lost boyhood. She must
think she can brush off time with dust
from model aeroplanes. I laugh it off in self defence,
who have come for a weekend to state my permanence.

Peace to unpack – but I found none
in this spare room which once contained you. (Dun-
coloured walls, one small window which used to frame
your old horizons.) What can I blame
for my unrest, insomnia? Persistent fear
elbows me, embedded deeply here
in an outgrown bed. (Narrow, but no narrower
than the single bed we sometimes share.)
On every side you grin gilt edged from long-discarded selves
(but where do I fit into the picture?) Your bookshelves

are crowded with previous prizes, a selection
of plots grown thin. Your egg collection
shatters me – that now you have no interest
in. (You just took one from each, you never wrecked a nest,
you said.) Invited guest among abandoned objects,
        my position
is precarious, closeted so – it's dark, your past a premonition
I can't close my eyes to. I shiver despite
the electric blanket and the deceptive mildness of the night.

SONG FOR COMING HOME

I browsed among the dress shop windows
(The town, the sun, the styles were new.)
I was looking for something lightweight for summer
And picked on you.

But what was less than love in summer
Autumn turned to almost hate.
So now I leave our bed of roses
With a hurt like a heavy weight.

I'm drinking beer in a speeding buffet
Along with some soldier I've met on this train.
My father will pick me up at the station
But I'll have to put me together again.

GEORGE SQUARE

George Square
idleness
an island
children splashing
in a sea of pigeons
pigeons strutting
pigeon-toed.

And we
city dwellers
sitting
separate
close together.
City dwellers
we only know
nature captive –
zoos and gardens
Latin-tagged.
We know no earth
or roots.
We see no slow
season shift
but sudden summer
blaze a concrete day
and catch us unawares.
We can find no sense
in traffic lights'
continual change of emphasis.

Nature captive:
this is a city
nature's barred.
But the flowers
bound and bedded
bloom
incurable as cancer
and as for fat old ladies'
flowery
summer dresses
my god they really are
a riot.

MAN ON A BENCH

This old man
has grown year-weary
no joy in changing seasons, just
another blooming spring
another sodden summer
another corny old autumn
and another winter
to leave him cold.

CARNIVAL

Glass roof holds down a
stale air of excitement,
bottles up noise.
It's all screams and legs
cutting prescribed arcs. We walk,
the lights revolve around you.
People spin at tangents,
swing limit-wards on chain end.
Collisions are less than inevitable.

The speedway is a whirlpool.
The waltzer reels out-of-time
to ten pop songs.
Pressures force skirts up, girls bare
their teeth and scream.
You say it's screams of pleasure.
The timid roll pennies.

Aunt Sally has ten men. They
grin and shake their heads.
I miss the point.
The hall of mirrors hints at all sorts
of horrible distortions, but
you're favourably reflected in my eyes.
We play the fruit machines.

I spin to a mere blur on a wheelspoke
about your axis. There is a smell of onions
and axle grease.
The ghost train has pop-up fears for fun,
makes me laugh off mine and try
octopus, big dipper, roller coaster.
(Single riders pay double fare.)

Here is no plain sailing, all bump
and jerk. Above the screams, the sound
of some clown laughing.
Showmen shuffle hoops, push darts.
Prizes are sheer trash, and every lady wins.
You buy me candyfloss and smile.
I sink my teeth into sweet damn all.

CLOAKROOM

Firstly
you girls who are younger
and therefore more hopeful,
thinking this is Woman's Own World
and that a dab of such and such
perfume behind the ears
will lure
a kid-gloved dream lover
who knows how to treat a girl
gently.
You think you can tangle him in your curls
and snare him with your fishnet
stockings.

Secondly
we girls who are older
and therefore – but *is* it wiser
to recognise our failure
reflected in succeeding Saturday nights?
Our eyes are blank
of illusions
but we automatically
lengthen lashes, lacquer hair
lipstick our lips for later
and the too easily faked closeness
of close-mouth kisses
which always
leave a lot to be desired.

THE CHOOSING

We were first equal Mary and I
with same coloured ribbons in mouse-coloured hair
and with equal shyness,
we curtseyed to the lady councillor
for copies of Collins' Children's Classics.
First equal, equally proud.

Best friends too Mary and I
a common bond in being cleverest (equal)
in our small school's small class.
I remember
the competition for top desk
at school service.
And my terrible fear
of her superiority at sums.

I remember the housing scheme
where we both stayed.
The same houses, different homes,
where the choices were made.

I don't know exactly why they moved,
but anyway they went.
Something about a three-apartment
and a cheaper rent.
But from the top deck of the high-school
bus I'd glimpse among the others on the corner

Mary's father, mufflered, contrasting strangely
with the elegant greyhounds by his side.
He didn't believe in high school education,
especially for girls,
or in forking out for uniforms.

Ten years later on a Saturday –
I am coming from the library –
sitting near me on the bus,
Mary
with a husband who is tall,
curly haired, has eyes
for no one else but Mary.
Her arms are round the full-shaped vase
that is her body.
Oh, you can see where the attraction lies
in Mary's life –
not that I envy her, really.

And I am coming from the library
with my arms full of books.
I think of those prizes that were ours for the taking
and wonder when the choices got made
we don't remember making.

HOMILIES FROM HOSPITAL

There was a bit of an upset
one afternoon. Well, waking
from an after-dinner nap (you get so tired) I
heard sounds, moans I suppose you would call them,
small cries, a kind of
whimpering.
That Miss Galbraith it was her all right.
The curtains were well-drawn but
hanging down
below their floral edge (they're no longer than bed-level)
her half
     -leg cut off just below the knee
and a nurse with forceps or something
at the stitches.
It was loose
around the bonestump, like leather folded under, gathered
and hamstrung with catgut.
The skin was a bit on the blue side, oh
                           her
                           shrieks and three
loud dark drops of bad blood
from where the clean thing had probed it.
Of course all this was none
too pleasant
for anyone concerned. But on the whole here
it's a well-ordered existence.
Daily
those of us who are up to it, fix the flowers.
(Daffodils are in season make a fine show for

the visiting hour).
There's not much to it to tell the truth
it's just a matter of the fresh ones
arranging them as best you can and
picking out the dead ones
then disposing of them in the polythene sack in the slunge
which smells a bit.
This is only natural.

I had my dressing changed today.
To be honest I had not thought to be flawed
so very visibly.
But when all is said and done, no matter.
Getting better is the main thing.

Up and about again. The world
shrinks to the size of the ward
and this dull day room.
Weak sun and one day much like
any other. We are on Christian name terms
in no time.
Newspapers come, full of nonsense
BLIND CLIMBING ACE TO WED
EX-ORANGE CHIEF ACCUSED.
We are recovering.
You could call this a breathing space,
a chance to catch up on last Christmas's
correspondence.

But for the most part
looking out of the window
at the stray sheep in the hospital grounds
making themselves ill
silly creatures
cropping in the rhubarb patch, is about all we are good for.
We all agree operations
fairly take it out of you.
There is a TV we don't watch much.
We cannot laugh / we are in stitches.
The way we feel
a sneeze would split us at the seam. Oh,
but our wounds won't gape unless we are unwise &
overdo things.
We are reminded healing hurts.
We all have wounds

which will

get better through time, the marks
fade into ferns like fossils,
become old wounds.
All in all most of us are making good
recoveries. With luck we'll be home soon,
back to our loved ones
(oh and here's hoping)
because they love us they will also
love our scars.

OBJECT

I, love,
am capable of being looked at
from many different angles. This
is your problem.
In this cold north light it may
seem clear enough.
You pick your point of view
and stick to it, not veering much –
this
being the only way to make any sense of me
as a formal object. Still
I do not relish it, being
stated so – my edges defined
elsewhere than I'd imagined them
with a crispness I do not possess.

The economy of your line does not spare me
by its hairsbreadth.
I am limited. In whose likeness
do you reassemble me?
It's a fixed attitude you
force me into.
Cramp knots calf muscles;
pins and needles rankle in my arm;
my shoulder aches;
irked, I am aware of my extremities.
A casual pose, at first it seemed
quite natural. My features freeze.
A snapshot's decision would have demanded nothing

much of me in the way of endurance.
Perhaps your eye's lens, being selective, is more merciful?
It flicks
constantly between us, taking stock,
trying to see me in proper proportion.
I did not choose which face to confront you with.

As a diversion
my eyes are allowed just this
wedge of studio and window space
over your left shoulder
and above your head.

Over and over, indifferent,
my boredom records it, raw and formless,
studio clutter
the floorboards' irregularities
a knot or two
occasional splinters going against the grain;
Random spatters on the white wall –
cerulean, terre verte,
transparent golden ochre; black
dust on white ledge; chestnut tree's topmost
pale candles flickering beyond the sill,
cutting the clean edge of the attic opposite;
(once, over there, mirrored,
seen at several removes if I strained my eyes enough,
a woman in an overall
entering that dim room and
later leaving again, shutting out a square of light).
The thin wisps of smoke from those strange-shaped chimney

pots, the innumerable tones of grey
and green-grey merging, Spring glimmering.

In this view of things
too much to take into account is what it amounts to:
But you, love,
set me down in black and white exactly.
I am at once
reduced and made more of.

WEDDING MARCH

Could I buy a white dress and hope for good weather?
Could I take something borrowed? Could we bind us together?
And while Visions of Sugar Plums danced in each head,
could we lie long content on the bed that we'd made?

No, I've not my own house in order enough
to ever make you a tidy wife.
Could I learn to waste not and want not –
make soup from bones,
save wool scraps, bake scones
from sour milk? Would I ask for more
than to lunch alone on what's left over from the night before?
Could I soothe our children's night time bad dream fear
with nursery rhymes, and never find my cupboard bare?
Imagine an old handbag full of photographs,
once in a blue moon I'd drag them out for laughs –
smiling at poses I once carefully arranged,
in hoots at the hemlines and how we've changed.

We'll try. It still is early days.
I'll try and mend my sluttish ways.
We'll give our kitchen a new look –
a lick of paint, a spice rack, and a recipe book.
I'll watch our tangled undies bleaching clean
in the humdrum of the laundromat machine.
I'll take my pet dog vacuum on its daily walk through rooms,
and knowing there is no clean sweep,
keep busy still with brooms.

RIDDLE-ME-REE

My first is in life (not contained within heart)
My second's in whole but never in part.
My third's in forever, but also in vain.
My last's in ending, why not in pain?

is love the answer?

MEMO TO MYSELF FOR SPRING

April
April first you must fool me
I am no longer
anybody's fool.
I have danced with too many
velvet tongued men.
I have seen too many
plaster effigies of saints
for faith to mean much.
Hope
is treacherous
and much to be guarded against in April.
I refuse to put out with
any more charity –
I won't be as mad as March in April.
April you confidence trickster,
you very practical
practical joker –
your clichéd burgeoning and budding
calculated
to set me wandering in a forest of cosmetic counters'
lyric poetry.
You urge me,
buy a lipstick
treat yourself to a new dress
try again.
But April first you must fool me.
April
I fear you
May.